Speakers' Club

Public Speaking for Young People

Written by **Barbara Juskow**   Illustrated by **Jean Thornley**

Prufrock Press, Inc.
P.O. Box 8813
Waco, Texas 76714-8813
(800) 998-2208
Fax (800) 240-0333
http://www.prufrock.com

Contents

Information for the Instructor

The ability to give an effective verbal presentation is an important skill. To be able to give strong, organized oral presentations increases a person's chances of being regarded as knowledgeable, capable, and in command. *Speakers' Club* is a series of lessons that builds proficiency in public speaking. In each lesson practical ideas introduce and reinforce the need for preparation and attention to detail. The series of lessons begins with fun, low-anxiety activities. As students gain poise and self-confidence, the tasks become longer and more difficult. By the end of the unit, students should be able to organize and deliver a two to four-minute speech that incorporates the main elements of good speech writing and presentation. In addition to developing speaking skills, the learning experiences in the *Speakers' Club* build self-confidence and leadership skills.

This program has been designed so that the culminating activity at the end of the unit is a luncheon where each student will make an oral presentation. This is an important part of this program as it presents a public forum for students' efforts and skill development. Students should be informed of this final activity at the beginning of the unit so they can be preparing for this event.

The following are the general topics that are presented in the lessons. Each activity includes a sample to study or evaluate before students are required to write or practice the technique.

- **Introductions** teach students the physical aspects of how to act and what to say when they have been asked to introduce a speaker. These lessons also teach the specific parts of an introduction and develop self-improvement by learning how to evaluate an introduction.

- **Quick-Pick Speeches** show students how to organize their thoughts into a cohesive unit by using a quick mental framework. Students will be asked to give three of these speeches. These quick speeches will give them their first opportunities to practice the various techniques that are presented. These speeches are short, do not require a lot of preparation, and are not evaluated in the same way that longer speeches are.

- **Writing a Speech** establishes the steps necessary in the preparation of a longer presentation and the practice required before public delivery of the speech. Students will learn that a speech has three parts (beginning, middle and closing) that deal with the main topic and follow a smooth, logical transition from one part to another. Students are also provided with speech evaluation forms so they can evaluate their progress. As they listen for specific parts in the framework of a speech, they internalize the lessons of speech writing.

- **Speaking Techniques** teaches students techniques for giving a more animated, audience-involved presentation. They learn how to use eye-contact, word emphasis and gestures to add drama to their speech giving.

Skills

Skills that students will be practicing as they prepare and deliver their speeches are:

- creative writing
- observation
- organization
- voice control
- group interaction
- risk-taking
- fluency
- flexibility
- originality
- elaboration
- evaluation
- research

Evaluation

There are several opportunities for evaluation in this unit. This program is designed so that after each of the three longer speeches students deliver to their classmates, they will evaluate each other. There are four different evaluation forms provided, each one reflecting the new skills that have been introduced. You may decide to use peer evaluations or not, depending on the maturity and cohesiveness of your group. It is important that students receive positive reinforcement and suggestions for improvement; so whether you use peer evaluations or not, you should evaluate each student's speech. You may wish to limit your comments to just one or two main criticisms so the student can focus on a few improvements for the next speech. You should, however, expect growth and grade presentations at the end of the course of study more critically than those presented at the beginning. It is expected that students will not only gain presentation skills but also poise and polish as they practice public speaking. In addition to having classmates evaluate each speaker, each speaker should do a self-evaluation. This is best accomplished by video taping the speeches and having students do a self-evaluation when they view the video of their speeches.

Other Opportunities for Speaking

Once students become skillful and confident in public speaking, you will find many opportunities for them to use these skills. There are opportunities for oral presentations in all areas of the curriculum. Some activities that would reinforce public speaking skills are oral book reports, reader's theater, discussion groups, oral reports in content areas, poster talks, interviews, demonstrations or explanations of how to do something, brainstorming, debates, plays, teaching a lesson, dramatic or expressive reading, or role playing. The more opportunities students have to develop and practice public speaking skills, the more comfortable they will be in making public oral presentations. The *Speakers' Club* is just the beginning. Throughout their lives, students will find a multitude of opportunities to share their ideas orally with other people. These other opportunities may not require the formal presentations that the *Speakers' Club* does, but students will draw upon the skills they learned in this unit of study.

Lesson Outline

This teaching unit includes plans for 14 lessons, 3 organizational sessions, and a final luncheon. The lessons are arranged to provide an orderly, developmental progression of skills. This organization allows students the opportunity to focus on only one skill or speaking technique at a time and master that skill before trying to integrate other skills. Each lesson includes all the information you need to present to your students as well as directions for student activities and worksheets. Depending on the time you have scheduled for this unit, you may want to combine some lessons. The information and activities presented in each lesson are as follows:

Lesson	Information Pages	Worksheets	Activities
Introduction	Course Overview		
1			self introduction
2			introduce another person
3	Planning Successful Intro.	Rating Introductions	
4	Making Introductions	Writing an Introduction	write and deliver an introduction
5	Oral Book Report		oral book review
6	Organizing a Quick Speech	Outline for a Quick Speech	quick-pick speech 1
		Quick-Pick Topics	
7	Preparing Your Speech	Planning Your Speech	
	Practice Makes Perfect		
8		Evaluation Form A	speech 1
9	Making Eye Contact	Marked for Eye Contact	mark speech
			quick-pick speech 2
10		Evaluation Form B	speech 2
11	Word Punch	Practice Using Your Voice	practice phrases
		Planning for Word Power	mark speech
12			quick-pick speech 3
13		Evaluation Form C	speech 3
14	Final Touch-Gestures	Putting It All Together	practice with gestures
		Marked for Body Language	mark speech
15			prepare for luncheon
			rewrite speech
16		Delivering Speech Like a Pro	practice speeches
final			luncheon

Lesson Plans

Introducing the Speech Unit

Objective: Students will understand the expectations of this unit of study.

Procedure:

1. Discuss the following things with your group:

   a) This is a practical course. It will be of value for the rest of their lives. It will make them feel more confident about themselves and equip them for a strong leadership role during school and in the workplace.

   b) Each student will be expected to speak each time a speech is assigned. As the course progresses the presentations will become longer.

   c) Students will be responsible for a minimum of three full speeches and three short impromptu speeches.

   d) Part of the course will be learning to judge other people's speeches as a means of improving their own performance. They will learn to judge good and poor delivery of speeches.

   e) Students will also learn techniques that will make them look and sound like pros when they deliver their speeches.

   f) There will be a final luncheon. Each person will prepare and deliver a speech at the luncheon. Parents, grandparents, teachers and friends will be invited to hear the presentations.

2. Distribute an outline of the course with dates and expectations. Read this handout together and make sure students understand the nature and commitments of the course.

Lesson 1 - Self-Introductions

Objective: Students will deliver an impromptu self-introduction.

Procedure:

1. Explain to students that for their first speech they will be walking to the front of the room and introducing themselves to the audience (their classmates). They should first state their name. Next they may tell about their brothers and sisters. They should give their names and an interesting fact. The third thing they will do is tell about their favorite two subjects in school (not recess). Next they should tell about a hobby or special interest they have. Finally, they should tell about one of their positive personal characteristics. This should be a characteristic that makes other people like them.

2. Tape a copy of "Talk About Yourself" (next page) to the lectern so students can refer to it.

3. Have students go to the front of the room and introduce themselves one at a time.

Tape this to the lectern.

Talk About Yourself

1. Your name

2. Brothers, sisters - interesting facts about them

3. Your two favorite subjects

4. Hobbies or interests

5. The thing about you that makes other people like you

Lesson 2 - Introducing Another Person

Objective: Students will practice the physical aspects of introducing another person.
Procedure:

1. Introducing another person is usually the first role students are likely to be asked to do. Discuss and then demonstrate with a volunteer the following physical aspects of introducing another speaker.
   - face the audience
   - lead the applause until the speaker arrives
   - after the introduction, wait at the podium and shake the speaker's hand
   - leave the front of the room or sit opposite the speaker's path to the podium
   - be attentive during the speech; set an example for the audience.

2. Have students draw names or assign partners and jot down what they can remember about what their partners said about themselves during their self-introductions.

3. Based on this information, they are to introduce their partner as a potential guest speaker. At this point, they should be mainly focusing on the physical aspects of an introduction. They should include a few sentences of information, but they need not give an elaborate introduction. They should say, "I'd like to introduce (speaker's name)" and give just one or two additional pieces of information about this person.

4. After the introductions, hold an open discussion about the techniques practiced and about the student's feelings at this point.

Lesson 3 - Evaluating Introductions

Objective: Students will be able to evaluate introductions.
Procedure:

1. Review the physical aspects of introductions from lesson 2.
2. Review information on "Planning Successful Introductions."
3. Have students complete the worksheet entitled "Rating Introductions."
4. Discuss what makes each introduction good or not so good.

Lesson 4 - Writing Interesting Introductions

Objective: Students will write and deliver an interesting introduction for another person.

Procedure:

1. Read the following introduction to students:

   "Some things are real and some things are imaginary. Then there are those mysterious things in between that we can't seem to put in either category. Our speaker this afternoon is here to tell us about one of them. Please help me welcome Sam Brown."

   Ask them the following questions:

   Is this a good introduction? How do you know? Were you intrigued by what was said? Were you wondering what this speech was all about? Did you want to hear the speech?

   Explain that if all of the questions could be answered "yes" then the introducer has done a good job. Explain that in this lesson, they will learn how to write introductions that will peak curiosity and set the stage for an enjoyable speech.

2. Review the information on "Making Introductions." Read through the sample introduction (also reproduced below) and discuss variations.

Sample Introduction

"Good afternoon ladies and gentlemen. It gives me greatest pleasure to introduce the (first, second, main, etc.) speaker on the program this afternoon. The topic (is of vital importance, will make you wonder about, is timely and important, can change the way you think about, etc.). Please help me welcome (speaker's name)."

3. Have students draw names of other classmates to introduce. Using the sample above have them write a short introduction for the person they will be introducing. After they have written the introduction, have them practice coming to the front of the room, introducing the speaker and having the speaker walk to the lectern in preparation for giving the speech. The speaker will not actually give the speech. The only person who will speak during this exercise will be the introducer. They can use the worksheet, "Writing an Introduction," to plan their introduction.

4. Review the importance of the physical aspects of introducing a speaker.

Variation: An added twist can be given to this activity by having the students select topics and pretend they have a speech ready on that topic. The sillier the topic, the better. The class will loosen up if anyone is still feeling uncomfortable. In this variation, the person doing the introduction should include information about the speech topic as well as the qualifications of the speaker to speak on this topic. Some suggested topics might be:

- My talking goldfish
- How I convinced a space alien to do my homework
- Why my dog bites only female (or male) letter carriers
- The day I looked like an idiot
- My mother, the neat-freak
- No one knows this, but three mushrooms are growing under my bed
- I'll tell you the secret about how I learned to drive a car
- Understanding the importance of mud in this world
- I've decided I can trust this group completely, so I'll tell you the truth about myself.
- Cheating at cards is easy. Let me show you how.
- I finally found out where the water goes when you flush.
- I was asked to make a video with Madonna, and I'll tell you why I turned it down.

Lesson 5 - Writing and Organizing an Oral Book Report

(Optional Lesson)

Objective: Students will deliver an oral book review.

Procedure:

1. Distribute copies of the student worksheet entitled "Oral Book Report" and review the procedure for presenting an informative and interesting oral book review.

2. Have students present oral reports on books they have recently read.

Lesson 6 - Giving a Short Speech

Objective: Students will prepare and deliver a short, impromptu speech.

Preparation:

Prepare slips of paper with the quick-pick topics on them. Duplicate the quick-pick topics on separate strips of colored paper, cut them apart and stand them like turkey feathers in a jar. Students will draw topics at random. No one should be allowed to read any of the slips prior to selection, nor trade after selection is made. If a student chooses a yellow slip for the first quick-pick speech, he/she can be assured of a different topic for the second and third quick-pick speeches by choosing a different color.

Procedure:

1. Review the information on "Organizing a Quick Speech."

2. Have each student randomly select a quick-pick topic.

3. Give students a few minutes to organize their thoughts for the quick-pick speech using the worksheet entitled "Outline for a Quick Speech."

4. Discuss the importance of the audience providing an accepting climate by listening intently and giving the appropriate positive reinforcement (applause) at the end of each speech.

5. You may choose to have students introduced when they give a quick-pick speech or you may make these more informal presentations. If you choose to have introductions, assign partners and have students prepare brief introductions.

6. One at a time, have students deliver their short speeches.

Lesson 7 - Writing a Speech

Objective: Students will research, organize and write a longer speech using given guidelines.

Procedure:

1. Distribute and discuss student information sheets entitled "Preparing Your Speech" and "Practice Makes Perfect."

2. Discuss using an outline as a way of organizing information and ideas. If students organize their information in outline-form, the middle portion of their speeches should be limited to three to five main points. Each main point will have supporting details, information or examples. If your class is familiar with thought webs, it may be helpful to organize ideas in this fashion.

3. Discuss writing speeches on notecards (5" x 8") for easy reference during delivery. The speech should be written in letters that are large enough to be easily read. Cards should be numbered so that if they are dropped, they can be easily put back into order.

4. Assign a two to four-minute speech for the next class meeting. Have students select topics and begin writing their speeches using the worksheet "Planning Your Speech."

Lesson 8 - Giving the First Long Speech

Objective: Students will deliver two to four-minute speeches on topics of their choosing.
Procedure:

1. Draw names for introduction partners and have students write appropriate introductions for each other.
2. Have students give speeches.
3. Video tape all introductions and speeches.
4. As each speaker talks, have the rest of the group fill out Evaluation Form A. Collect the forms after each speech. If evaluating all speakers is too tedious, half the class could evaluate the even numbered speakers, the other half of the class the odd numbered speakers.
5. As soon as the speeches are finished, rewind the video tape and watch the speeches. This is a good time for each person to do a personal evaluation sheet.
6. Hand out all the evaluation sheets. Discuss the results.

Lesson 9 - Making Eye-Contact

Objectives: Students will mark a sample speech for eye contact. Students will deliver a quick-pick speech using eye contact.
Procedure:

1. Read and discuss the student information sheets entitled "Making Eye Contact." Discuss speeches students have given so far and whether many students made eye contact. Have students practice reading the nursery rhyme to a partner, making eye contact at the appropriate places.
2. Hand out the worksheet entitled "Marked for Eye Contact." Have students mark the sample speech for places where they feel eye contact is appropriate. Then have them compare their sample speeches with other students' marked speeches.
3. Have each student choose another quick-pick topic and prepare an impromptu speech on this topic.
4. Randomly draw names and prepare introductions.
5. When students deliver their quick-pick speeches, have them concentrate on maintaining eye-contact.

Lesson 10 - Writing and Delivering the Second Speech

Objective: Students will be able to write and organize a speech on the topic of their choosing and deliver the speech using eye contact.
Procedure:

1. Have students select a topic for their second speech.
2. Review the techniques for good speech writing and delivery that have been presented so far.
3. Have students write their speeches, mark speeches for eye contact and practice speeches.
4. Just like the first speech, pick names and write introductions for each other.
5. As students present their speeches, video tape introducers and speakers.
6. Evaluate each speaker using Evaluation Form B.
7. Play back the video tape and have each speaker evaluate him/herself.
8. Hand back all evaluation forms and discuss.

Lesson 11 - Word Punch

Objective: Students will mark a sample speech for word emphasis. Students will practice saying phrases and sentences using different patterns of emphasis to give different meanings.

Procedure:

1. Read the student information sheet entitled "Word Punch" and discuss.
2. Distribute the worksheet entitled "Practice Using Your Voice." Have students practice saying each phrase in the way that is indicated. If possible, bring in several tape recorders, one for every two or three students, and have them record their voices.
3. Distribute the worksheet entitled "Planning for Word Power." Have students mark where they would add verbal emphasis. Divide the class into small groups and have each person read their interpretation to the group. Compare how each person marked his/her copy.

Lesson 12 - Practice with Eye Contact and Word Emphasis

Objective: Students will deliver a quick-pick speech using eye contact and word emphasis.

Procedure:

1. Review the techniques presented so far, especially making eye contact and using a variety of speech patterns and volume.
2. Have students draw a quick-pick topic and prepare a short speech on this topic.
3. Assign introducers.
4. Have students deliver their speeches, this time using not only a well-organized format, but also maintaining eye contact and varying their voices.
5. If needed, review any part of speech writing and delivery that seems necessary.

Next Assignment:

Assign the third speech for next week. The emphasis will be on eye-contact and word emphasis. Ask students to be thinking about a topic for this speech.

Lesson 13 - Delivering the Third Speech

Objective: Students will prepare and deliver a third speech using eye contact and word emphasis.

Procedure:

1. Have students select topics and write speeches.
2. After speeches are written, have students mark their speeches to indicate where they will make eye contact or use word emphasis.
3. Assign introducers and allow time to write the introductions.
4. Video tape all speeches and introductions.
5. Evaluate all the speeches using Evaluation Form C.
6. Watch the video and have students evaluate themselves.
7. Hand out all evaluation forms and discuss.

Lesson 14 - The Final Touch - Gestures

Objectives: Students will practice using body language to communicate ideas. Students will mark a speech for body language.

Procedure:

1. Distribute and read together the student information sheet entitled "The Final Touch - Gestures."

2. Practice the gestures that are indicated on the bottom of this sheet.

3. Distribute the student worksheet entitled "Putting It All Together." Have students practice saying each sentence with the proper emphasis and providing appropriate gestures.

4. Have students mark the sample speech on the worksheet "Marked for Body Language" for appropriate places to use gestures.

Lesson 15 - Final Luncheon Preparations

Objective: Students will select speeches for their final presentation and rewrite speeches incorporating improvements.

Procedure:

1. Have each student choose which of the three speeches prepared so far he or she wishes to deliver at the final luncheon.

2. New introducers should be chosen for each speech.

3. Ask for two volunteers; one to welcome the guests to the luncheon and one to thank them for coming.

4. As a group decide upon the order of the speeches. Make a printed program that lists speakers, their topics and introducers.

5. Letters of invitation should be ready to go home. Arrangements should be finalized for a group-prepared lunch or lunch served at a local restaurant.

6. Each student should rewrite the chosen speech and incorporate any necessary changes based on previous evaluations. They should incorporate all speech techniques that have been presented.

Lesson 16 - Dress Rehearsal

Objective: Students will practice their final speeches.

Procedure:

1. Have the programs ready. The students should run the whole show, beginning with the opening welcome and the closing thank you.

2. The entire program should be video taped.

3. Students should evaluate their deliveries using the self-evaluation form entitled "Delivering a Speech Like a Pro."

4. Discuss the luncheon arrangements. Be firm about eating time and speaking time. Know exactly when the program will start and stick to it.

5. It's a good idea for the teacher to have made copies of the final speeches. Once in a while one of them gets lost or left at home.

The Final Luncheon

Objective: Students will deliver polished speeches for an audience of relatives and friends.

Procedure:

1. Appoint one or two students to act as hosts to greet the guests and hand out the programs.

2. Eat your lunches and enjoy the speeches afterward.

Speakers' Club
Course Overview

By taking part in this unit, you will learn skills and gain the confidence you will need to be a good public speaker. Here is a listing of the activities that are planned and the dates for each activity.

Activity	Due Date	Points possible	Points earned
Self-introduction			
Introducing another person 1			
Rating Introductions			
Writing an Introduction			
Introducing another person 2			
Oral Book Review			
Quick-pick Speech 1			
Planning Your Speech			
Longer Speech 1			
Marked for Eye Contact			
Quick-pick Speech 2			
Longer Speech 2			
Practice Using Your Voice			
Planning for Word Power			
Quick-pick Speech 3			
Longer Speech 3			
Putting It All Together			
Marked for Body Language			
Final Speech			
Total			

Planning Successful Introductions

Here is a list of things that you should do before introducing another speaker if you want your introduction to be as informative, intriguing and polished as possible.

1. **Find out about the person** — Talk to the person you are going to introduce. Know how to say the name properly. Repeat it out loud until you have it right. Never fumble with the speaker's name. It makes you look silly. If it's a really difficult name, write it down the way it sounds to you.

2. **Find out about the speech** — Ask what the speech is about. If she answers "Dogs," you'll have to find out more. Ask what special aspect of dogs she will be speaking about.

3. **Prepare the audience** — Your task now is to prepare the audience; to peak their curiosity without giving the speech away. Do not discuss the speech yourself, even if you happen to know more about it than the speaker. It is not your purpose as an introducer to impress the listeners with your own wit, wisdom or special knowledge of the subject.

4. **Set the mood** — If there are several speakers, your introduction should build a bridge between what has gone before and your speaker's speech. Decide if your speaker needs a mood of seriousness or a mood of relaxed good humor. The way you look and speak and the tone of your voice will be the audience's cue to ponder a deep message or to blast off into fun.

5. **Give speaker's qualifications**
   Avoid embarrassing the speaker by describing him or her as brilliant, witty or a good speaker. If these things are true, they will be apparent when the speaker speaks. However, it is helpful to inform the audience that the speaker has had education or experience concerning the chosen subject. Let the audience know that the speaker is an expert on the topic.

6. **Plan ahead** — Plan your introduction carefully. Be brief.

Rating Introductions

Here are some sample introductions. How effective are they? Rate them using the following criteria. Record your ratings on the rating score sheet.

Rating Criteria:

1. Made you curious. You would want to listen to this speech.

2. The right length. Not too long nor too short.

3. Set the right tone for the speech, either serious or relaxed.

4. Hinted at the topic but didn't give it away.

5. Showed the introducer had put some thought into preparing this introduction.

Sample Introductions

1. Good afternoon and welcome to our annual luncheon. My name is Anne Smith and I will be your MC and hostess for the first half of the program. I would like to extend a special welcome to Mr. Bart Cook and to the parents and teachers who were able to make it to this luncheon. Our first speaker on the program, like all the other speakers here today, spends most of her waking hours in school. In fact, you might say that school is children's work. Please help me welcome Sandra Wilson who will tell us about the importance of education.

2. Our next speaker is interested in sports and he has many heroes in the sports' field. Today he has chosen to tell us about one of them. Please give a warm welcome to Chris Stone.

3. Most of us spend some portion of our time wondering how things begin, or happen, or end. Our next speaker will address this very topic as she tells us how the world was made. Please give a warm welcome to Jamie Brown.

4. By the time children reach this grade they have become experts on many subjects, especially the topic of the next speaker's speech. Please help me welcome Jenny Clearwater who will tell us about the responsibility of baby-sitters.

5. We all have our wishes and dreams. Our next speaker is no exception. Please help me welcome Michael Trenholm who will tell you about his dream bike.

6. Our next speaker likes to travel to new places and see new sights. Today he is here to tell us about a fascinating place he has learned about. Please help me welcome Willie Cantskouski.

7. These days we are more aware about the ills and excesses that threaten our lives. Help me give a warm welcome to Sunita Mohammed who will tell us about the dangers of smoking.

8. Our next speaker is a person who has interests that range from the outer reaches of the universe to the inner core of the earth. Please help me give a warm welcome to Ashley Simpson who will take us on a journey of discovery.

9. Our next speaker on the program had some difficulty settling on a topic for his speech. Finally he found one that is exactly right for this occasion. Please help me welcome Ezekiel D'Palo as he tells us all about decision making.

10. Music and music festivals take up a lot of our next speaker's spare time. She is an accomplished pianist and she knows a lot about many composers. Today she will tell us all about one of them. Please help me welcome Roselle Ng.

11. We all cherish our friends. Life would be a dull, cold place without them. Our next speaker will give us her perceptions about friendship. Please help me welcome a friend and classmate, Cathy Frederick.

12. A few years ago not many of us thought that the world of technology would affect us so directly. Now we can hardly imagine a world lacking the convenience of so many mechanical devices that make our lives easier. Our next speaker is going to tell us what else we can expect in the future. Please help me welcome Cory Buckert.

13. Is anyone here interested in moving? Our next speaker has information about selling and buying a home. Please give a warm welcome to Corinna Stephanson.

14. Our last speaker is going to tell us about a real life experience that none of us would ever want to face, and most of us won't have to. Please help me welcome Charmaine Johnson.

Rating Introductions

Score Sheet

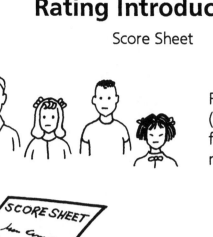

Rate each criteria on a scale of 0 (low) to 3 (high). Add the scores for the five criteria to get the total rating.

Person Introduced	Made you curious	Right length	Set the right tone	Hinted at the topic	Showed thought	Total
1. Sandra Wilson						
2. Chris Stone						
3. Jamie Brown						
4. Jenny Clearwater						
5. Michael Trenholm						
6. Willie Cantskouski						
7. Sunita Mohammed						
8. Ashley Simpson						
9. Ezekiel D'Palo						
10. Roselle Ng						
11. Cathy Frederick						
12. Cory Buckert						
13. Corinna Stephanson						
14. Charmaine Johnson						

Making Introductions

On Stage

Like a crowd at a play or a concert, your audience sits waiting for something to happen. They're chatting, a few late comers are finding their seats. There is a sense of expectancy. You walk up front and center. Eyes focus on you and the talking quiets. Like the orchestra conductor you are the one to start the program and you must do it right. Unfortunately you don't have a baton to tap on your music stand, so you must use other methods to get everyone's attention. Remember, they want to listen. That's the reason they're here.

What Should You Do?

1. Walk to the podium and wait.

2. Take a moment to make certain your notes are in order.

3. Look out at the audience. Try to catch several people's glance.

4. Stand very still. This says you're ready.

5. Smile.

6. Wait for quiet.

7. Begin to speak, slowly.

Getting Started

Every good introducer always has written notes to refer to. She may have every word memorized, but even experienced introducers have been overcome by nervousness. Having a written copy of your introduction will give you confidence and assure that everything will go as planned.

Start speaking slowly. Some introducers like to give their own name first. You can either say,"Good afternoon. I'm Susan Pollard and I'll be your MC for the speeches this afternoon." Or if you choose not to give your name, you might say,"Good evening. I'm very happy to be your MC for the program of speeches."

What Do You Say?

What you say to introduce the speaker depends on the person you are introducing, the topic he/she is speaking about, and the atmosphere (humorous or serious) you are trying to set for the speech. While you will be able to think of many creative things to say to introduce other speakers once you know something about them and their topics, a basic format that you might use as a guide when writing introductions is:

> "Good afternoon ladies and gentlemen. It gives me greatest pleasure to introduce the (first, second, main, etc.) speaker on the program this afternoon. His/her topic (is of vital importance, will make you wonder about, is timely and important, can change the way you think about, etc.). Please help me welcome (speaker's name)."

Remember that your primary function as an introducer is to prepare the audience for the speaker. You are not the highlight of the show, so do not play yourself up in any way. You are there to introduce the speaker in a thoughtful way, one that will be helpful to the speaker and to the audience.

Review

When you write an introduction for another person, remember the following things:
1. Be brief.
2. Spark the curiosity of the audience.
3. Set the right tone for the speaker.
4. Hint at the topic but don't give it away.

Writing An Introduction

Remember the following things when you are writing an introduction for another speaker.

1. Your introduction should have at least three sentences.

2. The first sentence greets the audience and mentions the speaker.

3. The second sentence gives a hint of the topic of the speech and tantalizes the audience so they will want to listen. Often a question works well here.

4. The last sentence says the speaker's name and welcomes the speaker to the front of the room.

Find a partner. Write a brief but attention-grabbing introduction for your partner. Your introduction should leave the audience anxious to find out more about his/her topic.

_____

_____

_____

_____

_____

_____

_____

_____

_____

_____

Oral Book Report

The ability to give an effective verbal presentation is an important skill. If you can do this, you will feel more confident and you will increase your chances of being asked to take a leadership role.

One of the best ways to develop self-assurance is through short speeches. You force yourself to think quickly and you learn to arrange the facts, observations and feelings into a cohesive unit. One of the things you will be asked to do repeatedly during your school career is to give an oral book review. This is a good exercise for organizing your ideas and making a brief presentation.

Organizing an oral book review

Think of all the books you've read. Mentally pick the one that would interest your classmates the most. Your immediate reaction might be to tell the group why you like this story so much, but don't start there. That's your punch line. Instead, begin thinking about all the details and special features of the story that make it so appealing. Ask yourself the following questions.

1. What is the story about? Is it an adventure? A romance? A slice of life? A humorous account of one person's struggles? A biography?

2. Who is the main character and what is the character's appeal? Why do you admire or feel a kinship with this person?

3. Think of one high point in the story and tell about it.

4. What makes you like this story? This is your ending — your punch line.

Something To Do

Choose a book that you have read recently. Use the questions above to help you organize a short review of the book that will make other people want to read the book. Write your presentation and then present it orally to your class.

Organizing a Quick Speech

When you give an impromptu speech, you don't have much time to write a speech. You must be able to quickly organize your thoughts in a way that will be interesting and easy to follow. Here are some guidelines that will help you organize your thoughts for a quick, impromptu speech.

1. **Start with a general statement of the topic.** Be positive and, if possible, funny. There's nothing like humor (if it's appropriate) to catch an audience's attention.

2. **Who is the person central to this topic?** The introduction of a person makes your topic personal and identifiable. Listeners like to sympathize with another person in an adventure or predicament.

3. **What is the most important aspect of this topic?** What is the most important thing you know about it? Present the main ideas in a clear fashion and support them with examples or facts. Use your words to create pictures in the minds of your audience.

4. **The ending is the most critical part.** It's the last thing to linger in your audience's mind. More than any other part, it will make you sound like a pro. End with your feelings or opinions on the subject. Say what you like or dislike or, if you can, make a suggestion on how to improve the situation.

Review

1. State the general topic or theme.

2. Involve or reveal a person connected to or interested in the topic.

3. Tell about the most important ideas and illustrate the ideas with facts or examples.

4. End with your perceptions or feelings and, if possible, your recommendations.

Organizing a Quick Speech

Example

Let's pretend that you have chosen to give an impromptu speech on one of your hobbies. You have only a few minutes to prepare your presentation before you are expected to get up and speak. This is how you might organize your speech. Since you would really only have a few minutes to organize your thoughts, you would probably only jot down brief notes instead of actually writing out complete sentences.

1. State your topic or theme

One of my favorite things to do in my spare time is to draw cartoons. I have several hobbies, but this is my favorite.

2. Reveal an involved person

While I really love to draw and my friends usually enjoy viewing my work, it sometimes causes me to have problems with older people. Ever since fourth grade my teachers have scolded me for drawing when I should be reading. My mother is always asking me when I'm going to quit scribbling and do my homework.

3. The facts

Cartoons are enjoyed by people in all countries around the world. They not only entertain and make people laugh, but many of them make important statements about people, politics and life. Cartoons are a way for people to laugh at themselves and see the amusing side of problems. Cartoon-like drawing is used to illustrate children's books and some text books. These illustrations make books and educational materials more interesting for students.

4. Personal feelings or recommendations

I think the funnies are as important as the news or the sports page. In fact, if I had my way, cartoons would be on the front page of every newspaper. I think it's better to make people laugh and be happy than it is to make them sad and worried. I am sure that you will agree that drawing cartoons is a worthwhile endeavor.

Outline for a Quick Speech

Use this outline to organize your ideas for a short impromptu speech. Since you will have only a short time to prepare your speech, you may find it easier to just write words and phrases rather than complete sentences.

1. General Topic or Theme _____

2. Involved Person(s) _____

_____

3. The Facts

_____

_____

_____

_____

_____

_____

_____

_____

_____

_____

4. Personal Feelings or Recommendations

_____

_____

_____

Quick-Pick Topics

If you went on a space flight, what personal items would you want to take along and why?

- -

Tell what you would like to do to become famous. Explain why.

- -

Tell about the neatest birthday party you ever attended.

- -

Describe one of your hobbies.

- -

Talk about ghosts. Tell all you know. If you don't know anything, make up something!

- -

How do you feel about telling the truth all the time? What troubles can be connected with this habit?

- -

Tell about your favorite relative.

- -

Give a description of your idea of the perfect family.

- -

In your opinion, what is the best holiday of the year. Explain what it means to you.

- -

Talk about rainy days and the best things to do when outdoor activities aren't possible.

- -

Describe your favorite T.V. program and give your reason for liking it best.

- -

If you could choose any unusual pet for your own, what would you choose? Why?

- -

Give a description of the nicest person you know.

- -

Tell what kind of animal you think it would be interesting to be and why.

- -

Tell how you would change the world if you had the power to do so.

- -

What is your favorite room in your house? Explain why.

- -

Tell what the job of peace officer is and then tell whether, in your opinion, they are doing a good job.

- -

Describe a person who would make a good group partner at school.

- -

If you could change your age, what age would you want to be and why?

- -

Describe the best piece of art you ever produced.

Adults can be a puzzle. Tell what you don't understand about them.

Describe the best story you ever read.

If you could surprise one of your parents with something wild and wonderful, what would it be?

Tell about some of the breakfast cereals you've eaten. Which one is your favorite?

Explain how new students should act when they move to a different school.

Tell about a time when you felt really silly.

What do you think have been the three most important discoveries made by humans so far?

In your opinion, what makes a person a good leader?

A recent survey shows that students have a lot of money to spend on themselves. Give you ideas on how to handle money wisely.

Tell which family position (youngest, oldest, middle) is best/worst and why?

Describe the qualities of a great teacher.

If you could take part in any Olympic sport, what would it be and why?

Give your opinion about TV commercials. Which do you think are the best? Which are the worst?

Discuss the best ways to make and keep friends.

If you could visit any part of the world, where would you visit? Explain why.

What do you wish you could learn in school and why?

What would you like to see invented and why?

Is television beneficial or bad for you? Explain.

What would your dream home be like?

Preparing Your Speech

Preparation Steps

Here are the steps you should take when writing a speech.

1. Choose a topic
2. Research and collect ideas
3. Organize the facts in a logical sequence
4. Plan the beginning and the closing
5. Write the whole speech

Choosing a Topic

The first thing you need to do is decide on a topic. Choose a topic that can be easily covered in the amount of time you have to speak. Generally, you should be able to state the theme of your speech in one sentence.

The topic of your speech should be your choice. Whether it's an important moral issue or a lighter slice of human nature, the best topics are the ones the speaker cares about. If the audience feels your enthusiasm and your excitement, they will listen.

Besides your own interests, you should also think about what your audience is interested in and expects to hear.

Remember that a speech has a purpose — to inform, to persuade or inspire, or to entertain. Decide on the purpose of your speech before you write it.

Planning Your Speech

A good speech has a beginning, a middle and a closing. Each part takes planning. One part should lead logically to the next part. All parts should relate to the topic.

· The Beginning

Your first sentence must wake up your audience and make them want to listen. The purpose of the first part of your speech is to introduce your subject and to get your audience's attention. The beginning sets the stage for the rest of your speech. Keep it simple but make it interesting.

· The Middle

The middle part of your speech gives all the details in an organized way. Choose a few main points. Explain your main points with examples, facts, anecdotes or illustrations. Cover your topic completely but avoid too many similar points. Try to find a balance between vague generalizations and overwhelming the audience with facts and figures. Relate each point to other points you have already presented or to the main theme. You may wish to present original ideas or suggest a new approach to the topic. Keep in mind the fact that you want people to be able to understand you and follow your train of thought. Don't use long, complex sentences or a lot of facts and numbers. If certain ideas are important, repeat them. Use vivid, descriptive words and phrases.

· The Closing

When you decide on the purpose of the speech, you automatically determine what the conclusion must be. If you posed a question at the beginning, it should be answered and your opinions should be clear. The closing may be a restatement of the main idea or a recap of the facts. The closing must sound definite and finished. End on a positive note.

Practice Makes Perfect

Every speaker, no matter how experienced, gets nervous before the speech is to be delivered; but if you practice your speech beforehand, you will find that you can deliver a polished speech in spite of your nervousness. The first step is to write a well-organized speech.

After your speech is written, you're ready to practice. This step is critical. Practice makes the difference between stumbling through a speech and making a smooth delivery. If you've gone to all the work of selecting a topic, gathering information and writing an entertaining speech, take a few more minutes and prepare for the delivery.

Practice Steps

These are these steps you should follow when you are practicing your speech.

1. Read the speech through twice out loud. This can be done in the privacy of your room if you feel awkward reading in front of other people.

2. Read the speech out loud again, this time in front of your mirror. At the end of every second sentence look up at yourself. You may wish to tape record your speech so you can listen to it. If possible, time the length of your speech at this step. Remember, people listen more slowly than you can read.

3. Now you're ready to read your speech to a sympathetic listener. Ask this person to offer helpful suggestions.

4. Now you're ready to stand up and deliver your speech. You can feel confident that you're well prepared and ready to deliver a stunning presentation.

Planning Your Speech

Fill in this outline with ideas you will incorporate in your speech.

Topic _____

Purpose of the speech ___ inform ___ persuade ___ entertain

Beginning

_____

_____

Middle

_____

_____

_____

_____

_____

_____

_____

_____

_____

_____

Closing

_____

_____

_____

_____

Evaluation Form A

Use this form to evaluate the speeches you will be listening to. Rate each item on a scale of 1 to 5, where 1 is the lowest score and 5 is the highest score.

Speaker's name _____ Topic _____

1. Introduction - Clear? Interesting? Captured audience's attention?   1 2 3 4 5

2. Middle - Well developed. Examples to explain each point.   1 2 3 4 5

3. Middle - The points are in logical order. The topic flows smoothly.   1 2 3 4 5

4. Closing - Definite, positive, thought-provoking.   1 2 3 4 5

5. Closing - There is a feeling the topic has been covered.   1 2 3 4 5

Comments _____

_____

- -

Evaluation Form A

Use this form to evaluate the speeches you will be listening to. Rate each item on a scale of 1 to 5, where 1 is the lowest score and 5 is the highest score.

Speaker's name _____ Topic _____

1. Introduction - Clear? Interesting? Captured audience's attention?   1 2 3 4 5

2. Middle - Well developed. Examples to explain each point.   1 2 3 4 5

3. Middle - The points are in logical order. The topic flows smoothly.   1 2 3 4 5

4. Closing - Definite, positive, thought-provoking.   1 2 3 4 5

5. Closing - There is a feeling the topic has been covered.   1 2 3 4 5

Comments _____

_____

Making Eye Contact

Why Eye Contact?

Writing a well-organized, interesting speech is the beginning of a successful presentation, but there are several techniques you can learn that will make your speech more lively and entertaining. One of these techniques is making eye contact. The best speakers make you feel that they're talking to you, not reading words from a paper.

What is Eye Contact?

Eye contact means looking directly into the eyes of different people in the audience. Do not look at someone's hair, tie or blouse. Do not look at empty chairs or out the window. And do not look at the same person all the time. Eye contact is a speaker's best tool to keep the audience interested. It says to the listener, "I'm talking to you. I see you. I acknowledge you. You and I are having a discussion."

Mark It

Making eye contact with your audience is difficult to learn. When you look up you might lose your place. But there is something you can do to help you know when to look at your audience and be able to find your place on the written copy of your speech again. Use a brightly colored highlighter and mark each spot where you plan to look up at the audience. In a short speech this may be only four to six times. In a longer speech it will be more. Usually it will be at the end of a sentence or the end of a paragraph.

Something To Do

Here is a familiar nursery rhyme. The places that are underlined are where you should look up at your audience. Practice giving this speech to a partner, making eye contact at the appropriate places.

Mary had a little lamb. It's fleece was <u>white as snow</u>. Everywhere that Mary went, <u>the lamb was sure to go</u>. It followed her to school one day, which was against the rules. It made the children laugh and play <u>to see the lamb at school</u>.

Marking for Eye Contact

Highlight the places on the following speech where you would look up and make eye contact with your audience. Compare your choices with your classmates' choices.

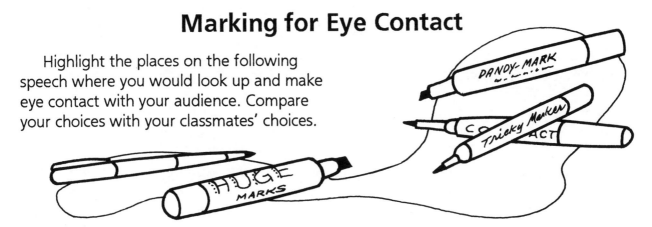

Choosing a Speech Topic

Don't you find that the first time you do anything in life, it's the most difficult time? I certainly do!

This is my first speech. It was to be two minutes in length, and it only took me seven days and seven nights of concentration and frustration to complete. Do you know how much junk food I've eaten this week while sitting around and trying to think of a subject? Do you know how much television I've missed? Do you know how many arguments I've had with my parents over the subject matter of my speech?

I immediately eliminated all the subjects I know nothing about like organic farming, the Renaissance in Italy, or how large canals are constructed. While I am sure that these subjects would be exceedingly interesting and informative, I didn't want to have do two weeks of research just to have enough material for a two-minute speech. Then, of course, there were the obvious subjects, such as "Earth Day" and "Our Environment." But two minutes isn't enough time to discuss something so important to all of us.

My family was really very supportive. They had lots of suggestions, but they also vetoed some of my ideas. I thought about talking about hockey, but my mom said many of you would not be interested. My dad tried to get me to discuss the will and estate of Harold Ballard; but, since his own children weren't upset by his great gift to charity, why should I be? Then my sister gave me some truly intriguing suggestions, such as "The Life of a Brownie" or her favorite subject, "The Life of a Hockey Sister." Since I rarely listen to my sister, I didn't want to start now.

Can you appreciate my problem? I've always thought of myself as a knowledgeable young fellow. So, how is it possible that for only two minutes I couldn't be an expert on anything?

One conclusion I have made is that I will never become a politician. Just imagine all that speech writing! I am hoping that my second speech will be a lot easier to choose and write.

Evaluation Form B

Use this form to evaluate the speeches you will be listening to. Rate each item on a scale of 1 to 5, where 1 is the lowest score and 5 is the highest score.

Speaker's name _____ Topic _____

1. Introduction - Clear? Interesting? Captured audience's attention?   1 2 3 4 5

2. Middle - Topic is well developed. Examples explain each point.   1 2 3 4 5

3. Middle - The points are in logical order. Ideas flow smoothly.   1 2 3 4 5

4. Closing - There is a feeling that the topic has been covered.   1 2 3 4 5

5. Closing - You have been well informed, persuaded or entertained.   1 2 3 4 5

6. Eye Contact - Made eye contact at the appropriate times.   1 2 3 4 5

Comments _____

_____

- -

Evaluation Form B

Use this form to evaluate the speeches you will be listening to. Rate each item on a scale of 1 to 5, where 1 is the lowest score and 5 is the highest score.

Speaker's name _____ Topic _____

1. Introduction - Clear? Interesting? Captured audience's attention?   1 2 3 4 5

2. Middle - Topic is well developed. Examples explain each point.   1 2 3 4 5

3. Middle - The points are in logical order. Ideas flow smoothly.   1 2 3 4 5

4. Closing - There is a feeling that the topic has been covered.   1 2 3 4 5

5. Closing - You have been well informed, persuaded or entertained.   1 2 3 4 5

6. Eye Contact - Made eye contact at the appropriate times.   1 2 3 4 5

Comments _____

_____

Word Punch

Using Your Voice

Your voice is a powerful tool. If you are not used to giving speeches, however, your voice tends to tighten and become monotonous and boring. With practice, however, you can learn to vary your tone and volume to make your speech more interesting. The most brilliant words are lost in a sea of yawns if the audience has to listen to a stumbling or boring delivery. On the other hand, the most ordinary words can elicit howls of laughter when given the right emphasis.

When you rehearse your speech in private have some fun. Turn your voice loose. Make an effort to make your words sound exciting. Practice talking slower than usual. Try to vary the rate of delivery. Vary the volume.

Mark Your Speech

You can be sure that you'll remember to vary your vocal style if you use a colored highlighter to mark places in your speech that need emphasis. Choose the words and phrases you plan to emphasize. The number will depend upon the tone of your speech. Reflect sincerity when you are sincere, humor when you're amused, emotion when you feel deeply.

Sometimes a pause can be as important as the words. Highlight the pauses you wish to make. Pauses give the listeners a chance to mentally digest what you've said.

Practice

You can have a lot of fun at this point with a tape recorder. Don't be afraid to use the various qualities of your voice; pitch, tone, volume, and even the rate. Stand up straight and speak out with enthusiasm. Don't be tense and rigid.

Practice Using Your Voice

Practice saying these simple sentences. Can you make them sound like they have different meanings?

1. **I** was born in Los Angeles. (You on the other hand, were born somewhere else.)

2. I **was** born in Los Angeles. (How dare you imply that I wasn't?)

3. I was **born** in Los Angeles. (I'm a native - not a newcomer.)

4. I was born **in** Los Angeles. (Not outside Los Angeles.)

5. I was born in **Los Angeles**. (Not in Moose Jaw.)

6. **Mary** had a little lamb. (Not me. I own a dog.)

7. Mary **had** a little lamb. (It was here a minute ago.)

8. Mary had a **little lamb**. (Not that overgrown beast.)

9. **He** hit me right on the nose. (Not someone else.)

10. He **hit** me right on the nose. (He did it deliberately.)

11. He hit **me** right on the nose. (I didn't start it.)

12. He hit me right on the **nose**. (A tender and special part of me.)

13. **I** had to drag her up the stairs. (I get all the tough jobs.)

14. I **had** to drag her up the stairs. (She wouldn't come on her own.)

15. I had to drag her **up** the stairs. (Down would have been a lot easier.)

Planning for Word Power

Use colored pens to highlight the words and phrases that should be emphasized. Practice reading the speech aloud with the indicated emphasis. Compare your choices with your classmates' choices.

Land of Strange Creatures

In what country are there birds that don't fly and fish that walk? In the far-off land of Australia.

Long ago animals could travel to and from Australia by way of a land bridge that connected it with other land masses. Later this bridge was covered by the ocean and the animals in Australia were stranded. From that time on, the animals in Australia developed independently from the animals in the rest of the world. That is why there are so many peculiar creatures on that continent; creatures that live nowhere else on Earth.

The most well-known of all the animals in Australia is the kangaroo. The kangaroo cannot walk. Instead it moves along in 20 foot bounds at speeds of up to 40 miles per hour. Adult kangaroos may stand eight feet tall, even though they are as small as one inch at birth.

Australia is not just the land of strange mammals. There are also birds in Australia that cannot be found anywhere else on Earth. One of them is the emu, a big bird that cannot fly. The emu looks much like the ostrich but is not quite as large as the ostrich. After the female emu lays her eggs, it is the male, not the female, that sits on them until they hatch.

Even fish behave strangely in Australia. The Australian walking fish uses its fins to walk out of the water and onto the beach. Sometimes it climbs trees in search of insects.

These are only a few of the strange and wonderful creatures that inhabit the unique country of Australia.

Evaluation Form C

Use this evaluation form to evaluate the speech you will listen to. Rate each item on a scale from 1 to 5, where 1 is a lowest score and 5 is the highest score.

Speaker _____ Topic _____

1. Speech organization - Clear, well-developed ideas.	1 2 3 4 5
2. Speech organization - Cohesive beginning, middle, closing.	1 2 3 4 5
3. Eye contact - Made eye contact at appropriate times.	1 2 3 4 5
4. Voice - Words clear, distinct and easy to understand.	1 2 3 4 5
5. Voice - Speed not too fast or too slow.	1 2 3 4 5
6. Voice - Used variety in volume and inflection.	1 2 3 4 5
7. Voice - Could be easily heard.	1 2 3 4 5

Comments _____

- -

Evaluation Form D

Use this evaluation form to evaluate the speech you will listen to. Rate each item on a scale from 1 to 5, where 1 is a lowest score and 5 is the highest score.

Speaker _____ Topic _____

1. Speech organization - Clear, well-developed ideas.	1 2 3 4 5
2. Speech organization - Cohesive beginning, middle, closing.	1 2 3 4 5
3. Eye contact - Made eye contact at appropriate times.	1 2 3 4 5
4. Voice - Clear, easy to understand, easy to hear.	1 2 3 4 5
5. Voice - Speed not too fast or too slow.	1 2 3 4 5
6. Voice - Used variety in volume and inflection.	1 2 3 4 5
7. Gestures - Used appropriate gestures and expressions.	1 2 3 4 5

Comments _____

© Prufrock Press Inc • *Speaker's Club*

The Final Touch - Gestures

Body Language

With the speech techniques presented so far (eye contact and word emphasis), you will be a powerful speaker. However, you may find it necessary to add a final touch — body language. Gestures and facial expressions add life to your speech. They make you seem like an energized, enthusiastic speaker instead of someone who is rigidly reading a written text.

Facial Expressions

Your voice and your face project your public image. When you're on stage delivering your speech, you are in the position of an actor. You are entertaining, educating or persuading an audience. But you are more limited than an actor. You must do it all with your upper body, hands and face. Good speakers can get an idea across with a roll of the eyes or another facial expression. Learn to use facial expressions to emphasize your words.

Gestures

Your hands can also help give visible expression to your words. Gestures require a good deal of skill. A good rule to follow is to use the right amount of gesturing to get your idea across — neither too much nor too little. If the sense of your speech requires movements to emphasize, describe, point out or express an emotion, use them. Gestures should be used only when they mean something.

Something To Do

Loosen up by practicing these simple gestures.

1. Point at your audience, at yourself, up, down.

2. Shake your fist in anger, excitement.

3. Hold up both palms to ask a question, to catch something.

4. Emphasize an important point by slapping one hand into the other or hitting the lectern.

Putting It All Together

Practice saying each of the following sentences with the proper emphasis or inflection as well as providing appropriate gestures.

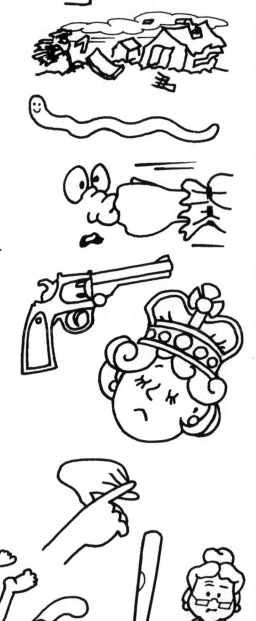

1. Here, take my hand.
2. The house was completely destroyed by the storm.
3. To whom can I turn?
4. I looked out over the prairie as far as I could see.
5. She pushed against the door, but it remained stuck.
6. I'm not going to tell you again.
7. Shh! Here comes the teacher.
8. Watch out! There's a snake.
9. She hit me right on the nose.
10. He reached for his gun.
11. Go straight ahead for two more blocks, then turn left.
12. Open! 'Tis I, the Queen.
13. Shame on you.
14. Let go of my arm.
15. Don't breathe this to a living soul.
16. He gasped for breath.
17. He swings a baseball bat like an old lady.
18. She took a deep breath and dove into the pool.
19. This means you, and you, and you.
20. If you keep this up, I'm walking out that door.
21. I spent two months of my life studying this!
22. This is exactly what I mean.
23. Do exactly as you're told.

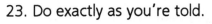

© Prufrock Press Inc · *Speaker's Club*

Marked for Body Language

Highlight the places in the following speech where you think it would be appropriate to gesture. Practice, then compare your interpretation with others in your class.

Inventions

Inventions are fascinating. Some day I'd like to create a famous invention of my own. Today, though, I'd like to talk to you about two inventions — Kellogg's Corn Flakes and Nestle's Toll House chocolate chip cookies.

How were corn flakes invented? In a very strange way, indeed. One day two mischievous brothers, James and St. Clair Kellogg, were experimenting in their father's machine shed. They put everything they could think of into their father's machines. Suddenly James had an idea. He thought they should put their unfinished breakfast through their father's dryer-flattener, a device he used to flatten and dry wet pasta.

They did it. And their breakfast, which had been corn and wheat mush, turned out a crisp, dry, golden brown sheet. James broke off a corner and tasted it. It actually tasted good!

They took it to their father who thought it was excellent. From that day on the two boys were famous. They had invented the first Kellogg's cereal, the well-known corn flakes.

And, how were Nestle's Toll House cookies invented?

Well, Mrs. C. Nestle simply thought the recipe for the Toll House Hotel sugar cookies was too dull. So she decided to enhance these cookies a bit by throwing in pieces of a chocolate bar. Wasn't that easy? She never guessed that they'd be such a hit. Everyone loved them. That's how the chocolate chip cookie was invented.

Inventions sometimes happen without intention. Maybe someday one of you will be famous for an accidental invention.

Delivering A Speech Like A Pro
Self-Evaluation

The best way to check your ability to deliver a speech well is to video tape it and evaluate what you see. Then you will be able to see what your audience will see. Check the image you are projecting by asking yourself these questions

Your Physical Image

___1. Are you relaxed but erect; not leaning on the lectern?

___2. Are you free of distracting things such as papers or jewelry?

___3. Are your hands used only for appropriate gesturing?

___4. Do you appear confident?

___5. Do you look up and smile?

___6. Do you use eye contact by looking at all sections of the audience?

Your Voice Image

___1. Does your voice have variety and a pleasing pitch?

___2. Do you use a strong voice that other people can hear?

___3. Are you using pauses to vary the rate and avoid sounding monotonous?

___4. Do you sound enthusiastic?

___5. Do you avoid inappropriate joking, slang or laughing?

Preparation

___1. Do you appear knowledgeable?

___2. Are you organized? Do you have all the materials you need?

___3. Do you know when you will use eye contact, word emphasis and body language?

___4. Have you rehearsed so you can deliver your speech in a natural manner?

Public Speaking Pointers

When you deliver an oral presentation, you will need to remember the following things.

1. Write so people will understand you.

Develop your ideas in a clear, easy-to-follow manner. Stay on your topic and present your ideas in a straightforward fashion. Limit your speech to a few main points and carefully explain those points.

2. Choose your words carefully.

Plan your speech carefully before you give it. Choose words that will be interesting. Paint a picture with words for your audience.

3. Body language is important.

Stand tall and do away with any habits or things that will be distracting. Appear confident, even if you're not. Use gestures and facial expressions to add interest to your presentation.

4. Establish eye contact.

Look at your audience. Look at people in all sections of the audience.

5. Use a strong, pleasant voice.

Emphasize certain words and phrases so you don't sound like you are reading out of a book. Speak loud enough so people can hear you.

6. Variety is the spice of speech.

Vary your pace (how fast or slowly you speak), pitch (how high or low), and volume (how loudly or softly).

7. Rehearse your speech.

Practice reading your speech out loud. Ask a friend to listen to it and give you helpful criticism.

8. Be organized.

Try to anticipate anything that you will need and have it ready.

Speakers' Club

Certificate of Merit and Membership

This is to certify that _____ has successfully completed all requirements to be a member of The Speakers' Club. Having developed the skills to be a successful public speaker, _____ is certified to be capable of delivering interesting, well-organized oral presentations and is awarded lifetime membership in The Speakers' Club.

_____   _____

teacher   date

Speakers' Club

Luncheon and Speech Presentation

Please join us for an afternoon of delicious lunch and stimulating speeches.

Date _____

Time _____

Place _____

_____

Speakers' Club

Luncheon and Program

Date:

←——————————→

Speakers and Topics

Common Core State Standards Alignment Sheet

Grade Level	Common Core State Standards in ELA-Literacy
Grade 4	SL.4.4 Report on a topic or text, tell a story, or recount an experience in an organized manner, using appropriate facts and relevant, descriptive details to support main ideas or themes; speak clearly at an understandable pace.
	SL.4.5 Add audio recordings and visual displays to presentations when appropriate to enhance the development of main ideas or themes.
Grade 5	SL.5.4 Report on a topic or text or present an opinion, sequencing ideas logically and using appropriate facts and relevant, descriptive details to support main ideas or themes; speak clearly at an understandable pace.
	SL.5.5 Include multimedia components (e.g., graphics, sound) and visual displays in presentations when appropriate to enhance the development of main ideas or themes.
Grade 6	SL.6.4 Present claims and findings, sequencing ideas logically and using pertinent descriptions, facts, and details to accentuate main ideas or themes; use appropriate eye contact, adequate volume, and clear pronunciation.
	SL.6.5 Include multimedia components (e.g., graphics, images, music, sound) and visual displays in presentations to clarify information.
Grade 7	SL.7.4 Present claims and findings, emphasizing salient points in a focused, coherent manner with pertinent descriptions, facts, details, and examples; use appropriate eye contact, adequate volume, and clear pronunciation.
	SL.7.5 Include multimedia components and visual displays in presentations to clarify claims and findings and emphasize salient points.
Grade 8	SL.8.4 Present claims and findings, emphasizing salient points in a focused, coherent manner with relevant evidence, sound valid reasoning, and well-chosen details; use appropriate eye contact, adequate volume, and clear pronunciation.
	SL.8.5 Integrate multimedia and visual displays into presentations to clarify information, strengthen claims and evidence, and add interest.